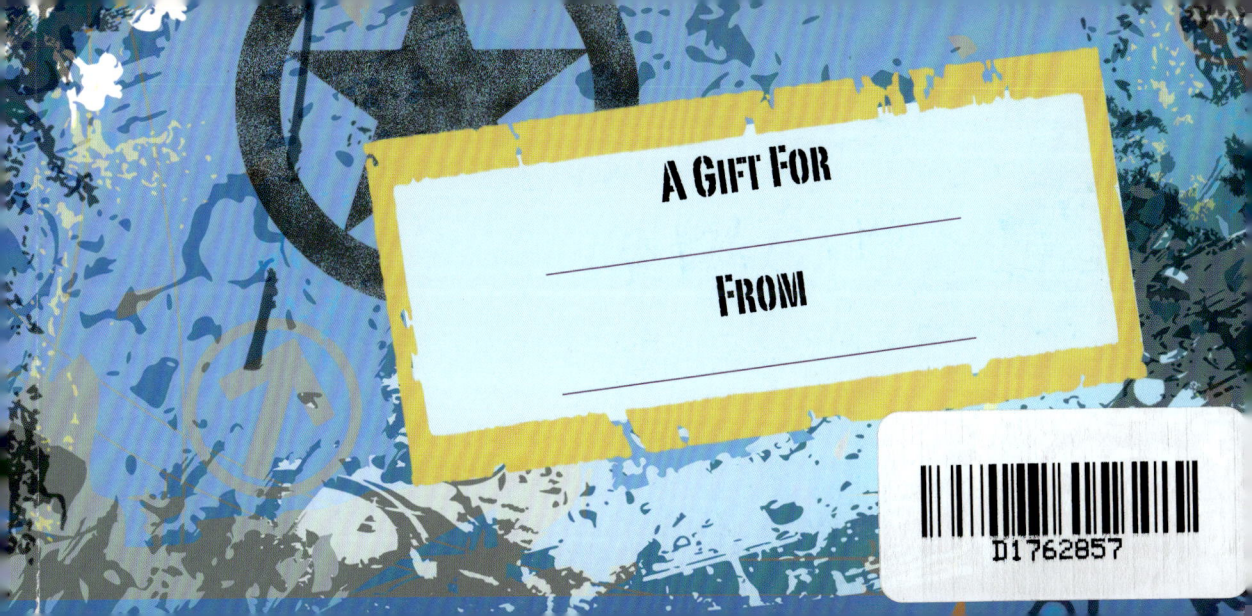

© 2010 by Barbour Publishing, Inc.

ISBN 978-1-61626-147-4

All rights reserved. No part of this publication may be reproduced or transmitted for commercial purposes, except for brief quotations in printed reviews, without written permission of the publisher.

Published by Barbour Publishing, Inc., P.O. Box 719, Uhrichsville, Ohio 44683, www.barbourbooks.com

Our mission is to publish and distribute inspirational products offering exceptional value and biblical encouragement to the masses.

ecpa Member of the Evangelical Christian Publishers Association

Printed in China.

For My Son

52 Creative and Fun Coupons to Show Your Love

BARBOUR
PUBLISHING

Good for one hour of

HEAD-TO-HEAD

VIDEO GAME COMPETITION.

Good for an afternoon of kite-flying...
or any outdoor activity of your choice.

Redeem for
one mystery activity.
(Prepare to be surprised!)

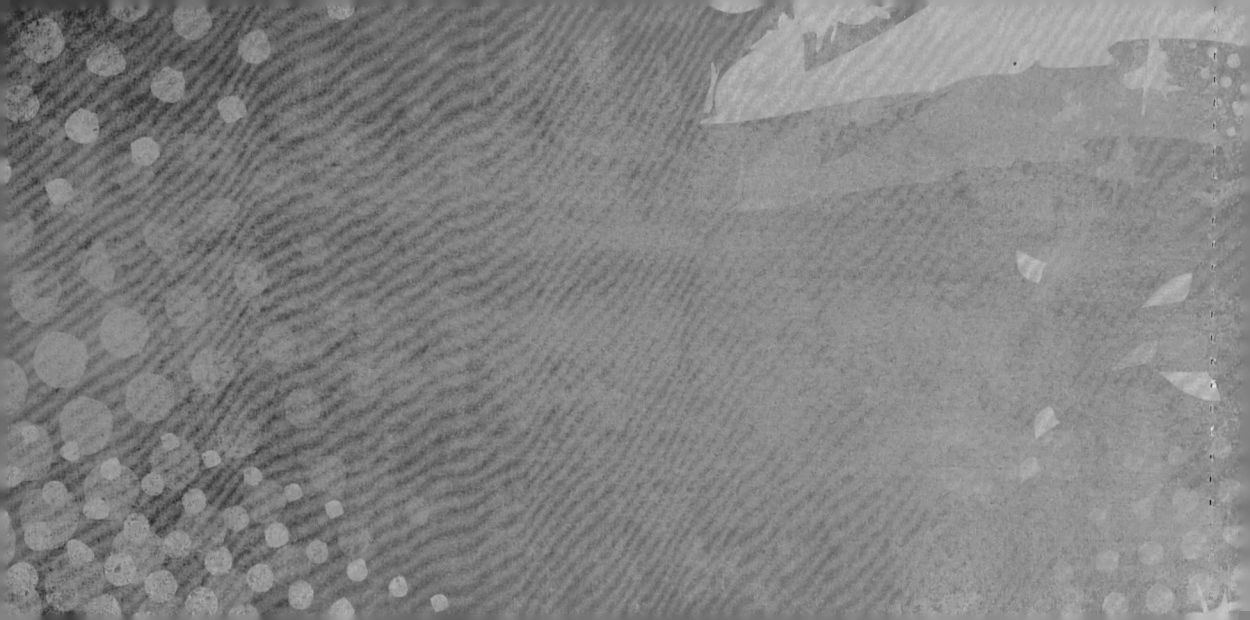

GOOD FOR ONE FREE
"don't have to clean my room today"
PASS.

Redeem for one lunch out— you choose the restaurant.

Chore freebie!

Redeem for exemption from one chore.

Redeem for a
poem celebrating everything **I love about you—**

penned by yours truly.

Redeem for your favorite snack.

(If we don't have it, I'll go buy it!)

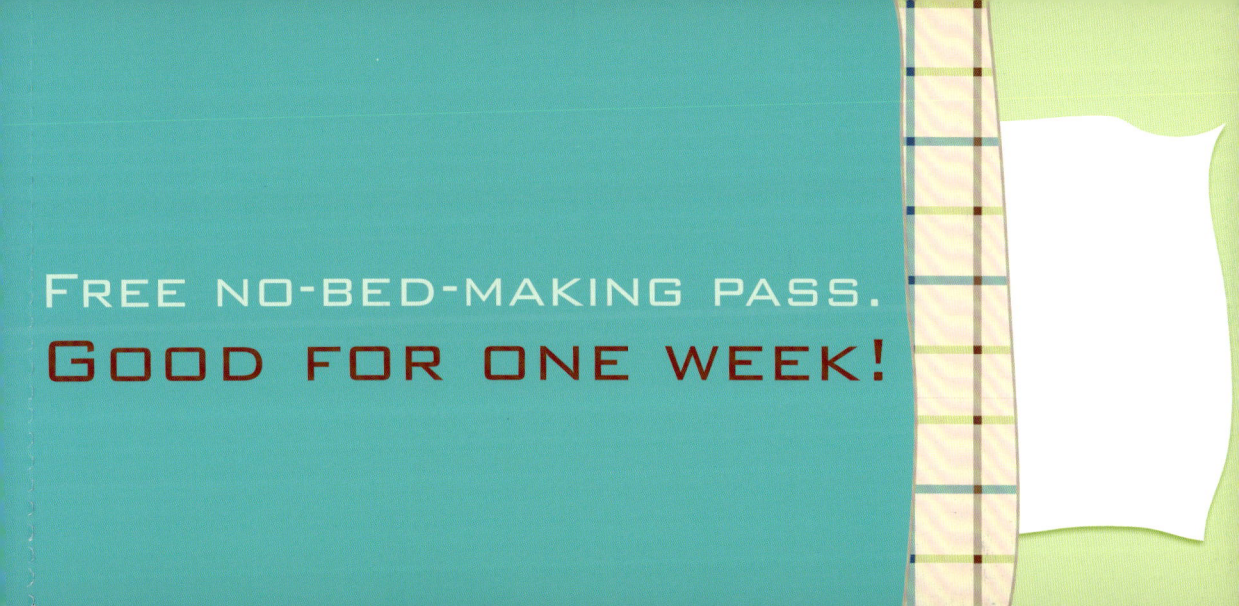

Redeem for the

DINNER MENU OF YOUR CHOICE–

complete with dessert!

Good for one
family movie night.

(You pick the movie, snacks, and time!)

Good for one
MOVIE OR VIDEO GAME RENTAL
of *your* choice.

Redeem for one "un-birthday" gift.

Good for one *family pizza night*—
you choose the toppings.

Good for an
afternoon of trying a new activity together—
horseback riding. paint-balling. . .whatever you wish!

Good for an
EXTRA ___ MINUTES
of **TELEVISION TIME.**

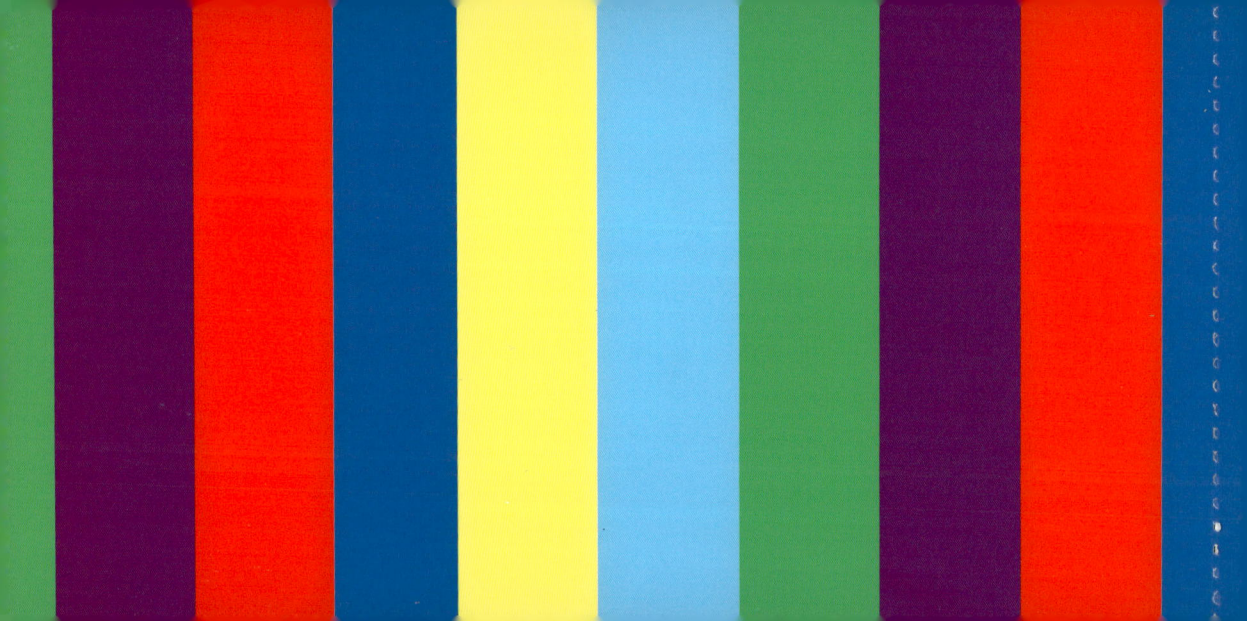

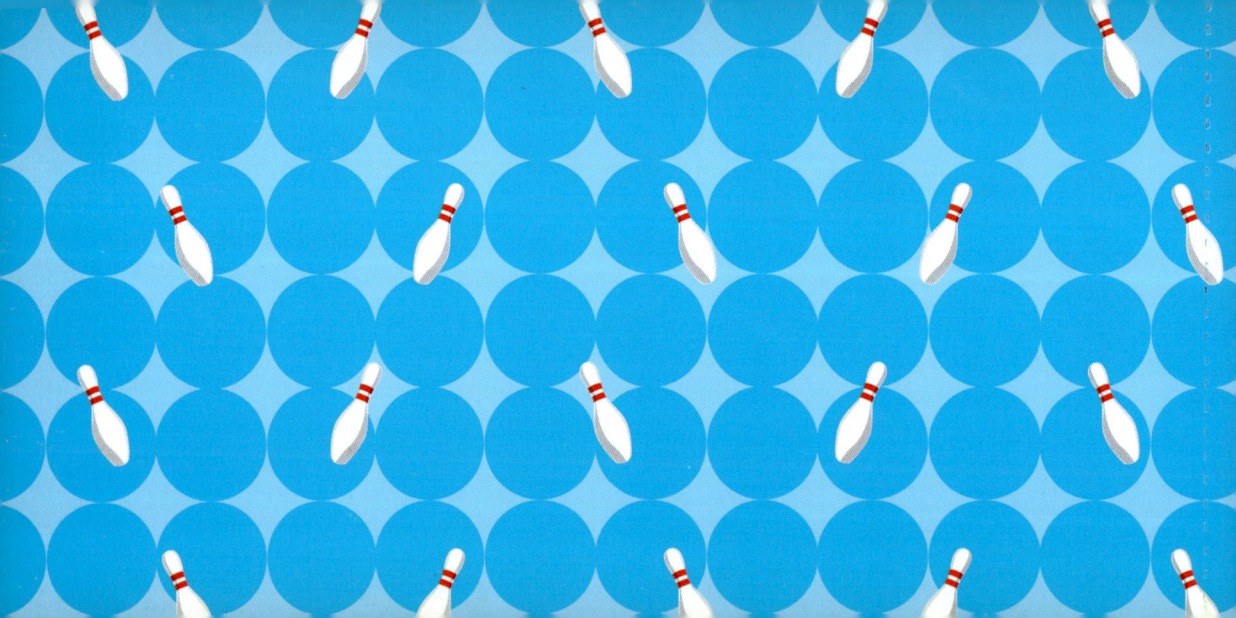

Good for one snowball fight—
with real or tissue paper snow.

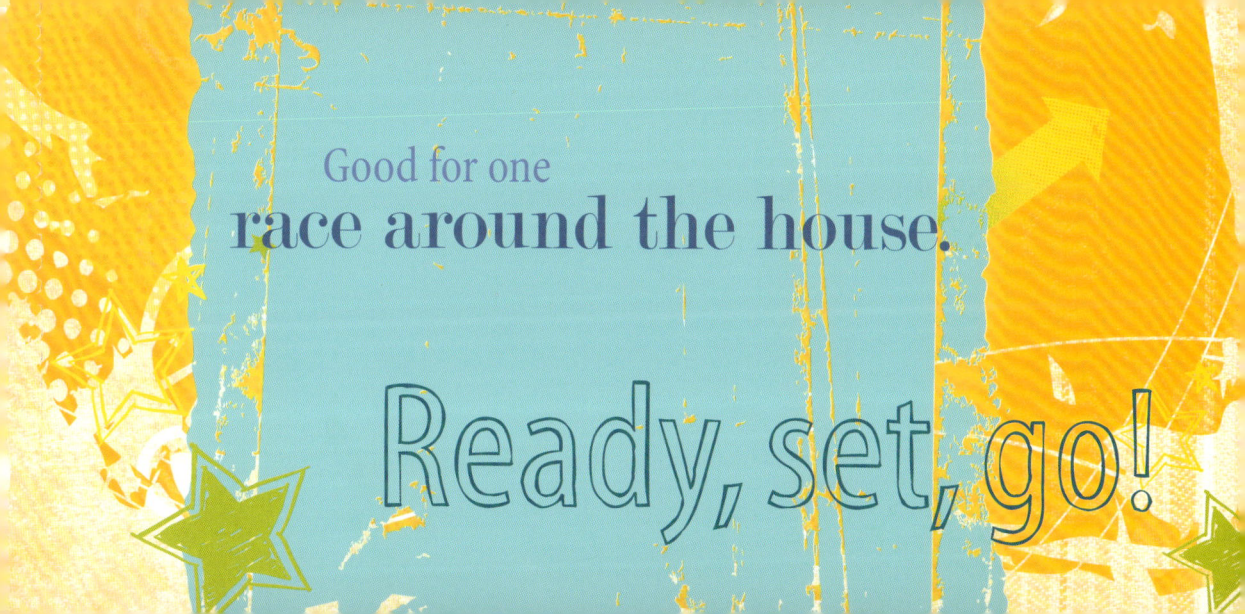

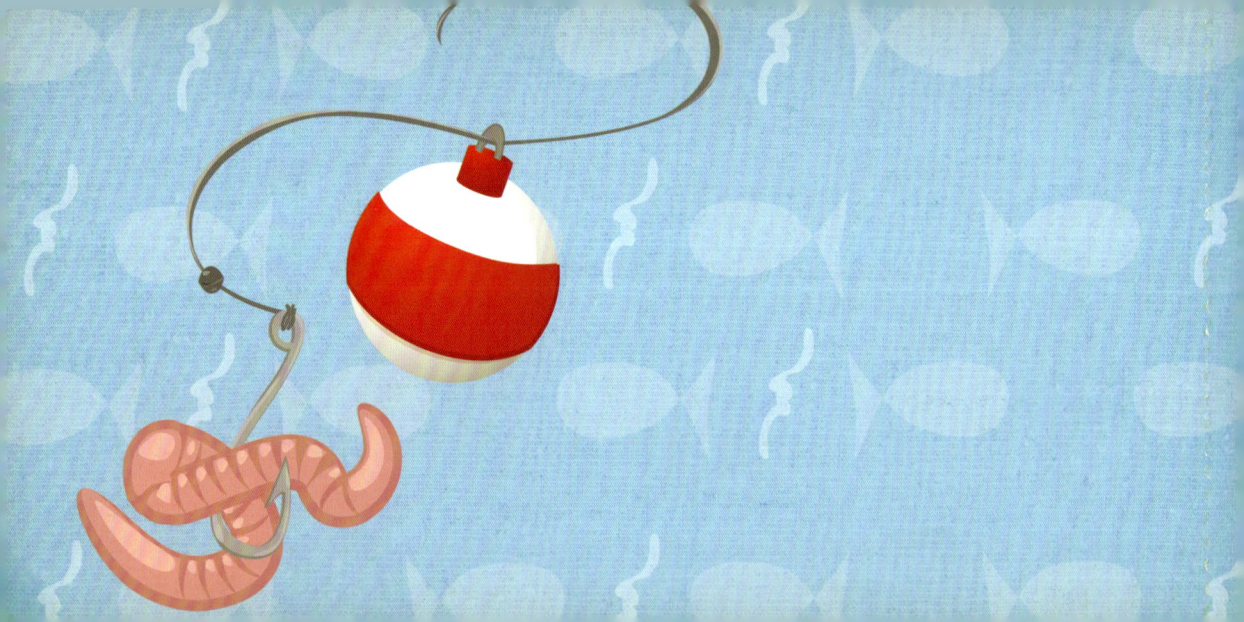

REDEEM FOR AN
hour of tossing
the football *with me.*
(GO LONG!)

Redeem for one afternoon
in the great outdoors—
hiking, bike riding, or another
activity of your choice.

Good for the
snack of your choice
prepared by your favorite chef—me!

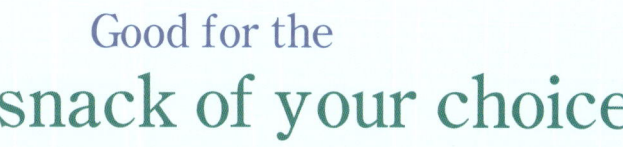

GOOD FOR

breakfast in bed—
waffles, pancakes, bacon, and eggs...
you pick!